# Decree

CONFESSIONS FROM THE WORD OF GOD
TO STRENGTHEN YOUR SPIRIT

# Decree

A thing and it shall be established

Job 22:28

By Patricia King

Belleville, Ontario, Canada

# DECREE

Copyright © 2003, Patricia King

*First Printing August 2003*
*Second Printing December 2003*
*Third Printing July 2005*
*Fourth Printing April 2006*

*All Rights Reserved. No part of this publication may be reproduced, stored in a retrieval system or transmitted in any form or by any means—electronic, mechanical, photocopy, recording or any other—except for brief quotations in printed reviews, without the prior permission of the author.*

The Word confessions in this book are based on the Holy Scriptures and have been adapted and paraphrased from various Bible versions. Where exact quotes are used, the New King James Version has been used.

Scripture quotations marked NKJV are taken from the *New King James Version*. Copyright © 1979, 1980, 1982. Thomas Nelson Inc., Publishers.

**National Library of Canada Cataloguing in Publication**
Coking, Pat, 1951-
  Decree : confessions from the Word of God to strengthen your spirit / Pat Coking.
ISBN 1-55306-706-1
  1. God--Promises--Biblical teaching. I. Title.
BT180.P7C63 2003      231.7    C2003-904476-9

*Guardian Books* is an imprint of *Essence Publishing,* a Christian Book Publisher dedicated to furthering the work of Christ through the written word. For more information, contact:
20 Hanna Court, Belleville, Ontario, Canada K8P 5J2.
Phone: 1-800-238-6376 • Fax: (613) 962-3055.
E-mail: publishing@essencegroup.com
Internet: www.essencegroup.com

www.extremeprophetic.com

DEAR FRIENDS:

The powerful Word of God is well able to profoundly influence your life. In Christ you have an eternal and unbreakable covenant. All of His promises are "*Yes*" and "*Amen*" (1 Corinthians 1:20, NKJV) to you!

Daily confession of the Word will strengthen your inner man and prepare you for every good work. The following are some reasons why the confession of the Word is found to be powerful in our lives.

### THE WORD OF GOD:

Is eternal in the heavens—*Matthew 24:35*

Will not return void—*Isaiah 55:11*

Frames the will of God—*Hebrews 11:3*

Dispatches angels—*Psalm 103:20*

Brings light into darkness—*Psalm 119:130*

Is a lamp unto our feet and a light unto our path—*Psalm 119:105*

Secures blessings—*Ephesians 1:3; 2 Peter 1:3*

Is seed—*Mark 4*

Is our weapon of warfare—*Ephesians 6;*

# DECREE

*2 Corinthians 10:3-5*
Pulls down mindsets—*2 Corinthians 10:3-5*
Creates—*Romans 4:17*
Sanctifies—*John 17:17*
Strengthens the spirit man—*Ephesians 5:26*
Ensures answers to prayer—*John 15:7*

May you truly enjoy a season of strengthening and may you be forever established in the manifestation of His glorious Word.

Visit our Web site at www.extremeprophetic.com or contact us by phone (toll free for Canada and the U.S.A.) 1-866-765-9286 or (250)765-9286.

In His victorious service with you,

*Patricia King*

# PRAYER OF DEDICATION

*Dear Heavenly Father,*

*I dedicate myself to You this day, in spirit, soul and body. Convict me of any thought, word or deed that has been displeasing to You. I ask for cleansing from all sin, according to the promise in Your Word that if I confess my sin then You will be faithful to forgive me and to cleanse me from all unrighteousness (1 John 1:9).*

*As I confess and decree Your Word, may Your Holy Spirit help me to be a passionate worshiper, a lover of truth and a faithful child who brings pleasure to Your righteous heart.*

*May I experience spiritual strengthening through the power of Your Word, for Your Word does not return void but accomplishes everything it is sent to do.*

*Grant unto me a spirit of wisdom and of revelation in the knowledge of Christ, for the glory of Your Name and kingdom.*

*In Jesus' name, I pray. Amen.*

*With my whole heart I have sought You;*
*Oh, let me not wander from Your commandments!*
*Your word I have hidden in my heart,*
*That I might not sin against You.*

—Psalm 119:10,11, NKJV

# DECREE
## PRAISE AND WORSHIP

Heavenly Father, I worship You in spirit and in truth. Along with the host of heaven, I declare:

*Holy, holy, holy, Lord God Almighty,*
*Who was and is and is to come!*
*You are worthy O Lord, to receive glory and honor and power;*
*For You created all things and by Your will they exist.*
*Blessing and honor and glory and power*
*Be to Him who sits on the throne,*
*And to the Lamb, forever, and ever!*
*Holy, holy, holy is the LORD of hosts;*
*The whole earth is full of His glory!*

You, O Lord are sitting on Your throne, high and lifted up, and the train of Your robe fills the temple. I ascribe greatness to You, for You are my God and my Rock. Your work is perfect, and all Your ways are just. You are a God of faithfulness and without injustice; righteous and upright are You.

I love You, O Lord my God, with all my heart, mind and strength. You are the Lord, and there is no other. There is no God besides You. I glory in Your holy name, and my heart rejoices in You. I will seek Your face evermore! I bless You, O Lord, my God. You are very great. You are clothed with honor and majesty.

# DECREE

While I live, I will praise You. I will sing praises to You while I have my being. The high praises of God will be in my mouth and a two-edged sword in my hand.

*Praise the LORD!*
*Praise the LORD from the heavens;*
*Praise Him in the heights!*
*Praise Him, all His angels;*
*Praise Him, all His hosts!*
*Praise Him, sun and moon;*
*Praise Him, all you stars of light!*
*Praise Him, you heavens of heavens,*
*And you waters above the heavens!*

**SCRIPTURAL REFERENCES:**

John 4:24; Revelation 4:8,11; 5:13, NKJV; Isaiah 6:3, NKJV; Isaiah 6:1; Deuteronomy 32:3,4; Isaiah 45:5; Psalm 105:3,4; 104:1; 146:2; 149:6; 148:1-4, NKJV.

# DECREE
## Everlasting Love

The Lord loves me with an everlasting love and has promised to give me a future and a hope. With lovingkindness He has drawn me unto Himself. I look carefully and intently at the manner of love the Father has poured out upon me. It is through this love that He has called me to be His dear child. I am completely and fully accepted in Him, my God and Savior.

Nothing can separate me from the love of God that is in Christ Jesus my Lord—not tribulation or distress, not persecution, famine or nakedness; not peril, sword, angels, principalities, powers, death, or life; neither things present nor things to come—absolutely nothing can separate me from the love of God which is in Christ Jesus my Lord.

God's love towards me is patient and kind. His love for me bears all things, believes all things, hopes all things and endures all things. His love will never fail. His love for me is so rich that He gave His only begotten Son. Because of this, I will never perish but have everlasting life with Him. As a result of God's great love for me, I have an unbreakable, eternal covenant with Him. Through this covenant of love, He has put His laws within my heart and written His commandments upon my mind.

# DECREE

I have been invited to the Lord's banqueting table, and His banner over me is love! His love is better than the choicest of wines. Through His intimate love, He draws me and invites me to follow after Him. I am fair and pleasant unto Him. I am rooted and grounded in His love, well able to comprehend with all believers the width and length and depth and height of His unfailing love. I have been called to know this rich love that surpasses knowledge, so that I may be filled with all the fullness of God. I truly am the object of His deepest love and affection!

**SCRIPTURAL REFERENCES:**

Jeremiah 31:3; 1 John 3:1; Ephesians 1:6; Romans 8:38,39; 1 Corinthians 13:4,7,8; John 3:16; Hebrews 8:10; Song of Solomon 1:2,4; 2:4; Ephesians 1:18,19

# DECREE
## Who I Am in Christ

I am a child of God; God is spiritually my Father.
*Romans 8:14,15; Galatians 3:26; 4:6; John 1:12*

I am a new creation in Christ; old things have passed away and all things have become new.
*2 Corinthians 5:17*

I am in Christ.
*Ephesians 1:1-4; Galatians 3:26,28*

I am an heir with the Father and a joint heir with Christ.
*Galatians 4:6,7; Romans 8:17*

I am reconciled to God and am an ambassador of reconciliation for Him.
*2 Corinthians 5:18,19*

I am a saint.
*Ephesians 1:1; 1 Corinthians 1:2; Philippians 1:1; Colossians 1:2*

## DECREE

I am God's workmanship, created in Christ for good works.
*Ephesians 2:10*

I am a citizen of heaven.
*Ephesians 2:19; Philippians 3:20*

I am a member of Christ's body.
*1 Corinthians 12:27*

I am united to the Lord and am one spirit with Him.
*1 Corinthians 6:17*

I am the temple of the Holy Spirit.
*1 Corinthians 3:16; 6:19*

I am a friend of Christ.
*John 15:15*

I am a slave of righteousness.
*Romans 6:18*

I am the righteousness of God in Christ
*2 Corinthians 5:21*

I am enslaved to God.
*Romans 6:22*

I am chosen and ordained by Christ to bear fruit.
*John 15:16*

## Who I Am in Christ

I am a prisoner of Christ.
*Ephesians 3:1; 4:1*

I am righteous and holy.
*Ephesians 4:24*

I am hidden with Christ in God.
*Colossians 3:3*

I am the salt of the earth.
*Matthew 5:13*

I am the light of the world.
*Matthew 5:14*

I am part of the true vine.
*John 15:1,2*

I am filled with the divine nature of Christ and escape the corruption that is in the world through lust.
*2 Peter 1:4*

I am an expression of the life of Christ.
*Colossians 3:4*

I am chosen of God, holy and dearly loved.
*Colossians 3:12; 1 Thessalonians 1:4*

I am a child of light.
*1 Thessalonians 5:5*

# DECREE

I am a partaker of a heavenly calling.
*Hebrews 3:1*

I am more than a conqueror through Christ.
*Romans 8:37*

I am a partaker with Christ and share in His life.
*Hebrews 3:14*

I am one of God's living stones, being built up in Christ as a spiritual house.
*1 Peter 2:5*

I am a chosen generation, a royal priesthood, a holy nation.
*1 Peter 2:9*

I am the devil's enemy.
*1 Peter 5:8*

I am born again by the Spirit of God.
*John 3:3-6*

I am an alien and stranger to this world.
*1 Peter 2:11*

I am a child of God who always triumphs in Christ and releases His fragrance in every place.
*2 Corinthians 2:14*

## Who I Am in Christ

I am seated in heavenly places in Christ.
*Ephesians 2:6*

I am saved by grace.
*Ephesians 2:8*

I am a recipient of every spiritual blessing in the heavenly places in Christ.
*Ephesians 1:3*

I am redeemed by the blood of the Lamb.
*Revelation 5:9*

I am part of the Bride of Christ and am making myself ready for Him.
*Revelation 19:7*

I am a true worshiper who worships the Father in spirit and in truth.
*John 4:24*

# DECREE
## VICTORY

I am a child of the living God. I am an heir of God and a joint heir with Jesus Christ. I am a new creation in Jesus; old things have passed away and all things have become new. I am a chosen generation, a royal priesthood, a holy nation.

I am not under guilt or condemnation. I refuse discouragement, because it is not of God. God is the God of all encouragement. There is therefore now no condemnation for those who are in Christ Jesus. The law of the Spirit of life in Christ Jesus has set me free from the law of sin and death. I do not listen to Satan's accusations for he is a liar, the father of lies. I gird up my loins with truth. Sin does not have dominion over me.

I flee from temptation but if I do sin, I have an advocate with the Father who is Jesus Christ. I confess my sins and forsake them, and God is faithful and just to forgive me and to cleanse me from all unrighteousness. I am cleansed by the blood of the Lamb. I am an overcomer, because of the blood of Jesus and the word of my testimony.

No weapon that is formed against me shall prosper, and I shall confute every tongue that rises up against me in judgement. My mind is renewed by the Word of God.

The weapons of my warfare are not carnal but mighty

# DECREE

through God to the pulling down of strongholds. I cast down imaginations and every high thing that exalts itself against the knowledge of Christ. I bring every thought captive into obedience to the truth.

I am accepted in the Beloved. Greater is He that is in me than he that is in the world. Nothing can separate me from the love of God which is in Christ Jesus my Lord. I am the righteousness of God in Christ Jesus. I am not the slave of sin, but of righteousness. I continue in His Word. I know the truth and the truth sets me free. Because Christ has set me free, I am free indeed. I have been delivered out of the domain of darkness and am now abiding in the kingdom of God.

I am not intimidated by the enemy's lies. He is defeated. For this purpose Christ came into the world, to destroy the works of the evil one. I submit to God and resist the devil. The enemy flees from me in terror, because the Lord lives mightily in me. I give the devil no opportunity. I give no place to fear in my life. God has not given me a spirit of fear but of love, of power and of a sound mind. Terror shall not come near me, because the Lord is the strength of my life and He always causes me to triumph in Christ Jesus.

In Christ, I am the head and not the tail. I am above and not beneath. A thousand shall fall at my side and ten thousand at my right hand and none shall touch me. I am seated with Christ in the heavenly places, far above all principalities and powers. I have been given power to tread upon serpents and scorpions and over all the power of the enemy, and nothing shall injure me. No longer will the enemy oppress me. I defeat him by the authority that Christ has given me. I am more than a conqueror through Christ.

# Victory

**SCRIPTURAL REFERENCES:**

Romans 6:16; 8:1,2,17,32,37,39; 12:2; 2 Corinthians 2:14; 5:17,21; 10:3-5; 1 Peter 2:9; John 8:36,44; Ephesians 1:6,20,21; 4:27; 6:14; 1 John 1:9; 2:1; 3:8; Revelation 12:11; Isaiah 54:17; Colossians 1:13; James 4:7; 2 Timothy 1:7; Psalm 27:1; Deuteronomy 28:13; Psalm 91:7; Luke 10:19

# DECREE

## WISDOM

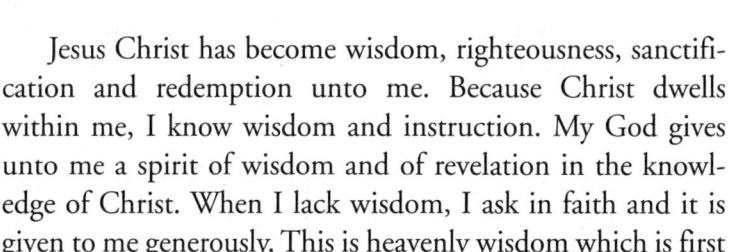

Jesus Christ has become wisdom, righteousness, sanctification and redemption unto me. Because Christ dwells within me, I know wisdom and instruction. My God gives unto me a spirit of wisdom and of revelation in the knowledge of Christ. When I lack wisdom, I ask in faith and it is given to me generously. This is heavenly wisdom which is first pure, then peaceable, gentle, easily entreated, full of mercy and good fruits, unwavering and without hypocrisy.

I discern the sayings of understanding, and I receive instruction in wise behavior, justice and fairness. I walk in the fear of the Lord, which is the beginning of knowledge. Jesus pours out His spirit of wisdom upon me and makes His words of wisdom known to me.

I receive the sayings of wisdom, and I treasure the commandments of the Lord within me. My ear is attentive to wisdom, and I incline my heart to understanding. I cry for discernment and lift my voice for understanding. I seek for wisdom as for silver and search for it as for hidden treasures. Because of this, I will discern the fear of the Lord and discover the knowledge of God. The Lord gives me wisdom.

From His mouth comes knowledge and understanding. He stores up sound wisdom for me. He is a shield to me, and

# DECREE

He guards my paths with justice and preserves my way. Wisdom enters my heart and knowledge is pleasant to my soul. Discretion guards me, and understanding watches over me to deliver me from the way of evil.

I do not let kindness and truth leave me. I bind them around my neck and write them on the tablet of my heart, so that I find favor and good repute with God and man. I trust in the Lord with all my heart, and I do not lean on my own understanding. In all my ways I acknowledge Him, and He makes my paths straight. I am blessed, because I find wisdom and I gain understanding.

I have long, full life, because it is in wisdom's right hand, and I have the riches and honor that are in wisdom's left hand. Because I love wisdom, all my paths are peace and my ways pleasant. Wisdom is a tree of life to me, and I am blessed because I hold her fast. I inherit honor, because of my love for wisdom, and my dwelling is blessed.

I acquire wisdom and understanding. I do not forsake wisdom; therefore, wisdom is my guard. I love wisdom and am watched over. Because I prize and embrace wisdom, wisdom exalts and honors me. Wisdom places a garland of grace on my head and presents me with a crown of beauty. I call wisdom my sister and understanding my intimate friend.

Because I love wisdom, riches and honor are with me, enduring wealth and righteousness. Wisdom endows me with wealth and fills my treasuries. I listen to wisdom and daily watch at her gates. I eat wisdom's food and drink of the wine that she has mixed. I forsake folly and live. I proceed in the way of understanding. When I speak, I speak noble things, and the opening of my mouth produces right things. My mouth utters truth. All the utterances of my mouth are in righteousness, because I walk in the way of wisdom.

**SCRIPTURAL REFERENCES:**

1 Corinthians 1:30; Ephesians 1:17; James 1:5; 3:17; Proverbs 1:2,3,7,23; 2:1-12; 3; 4:5-9; 7:4; 8:6-8; 9:5,6

# DECREE
## Provision and Resource

I seek first the kingdom of God and His righteousness, and all the things that I need are added unto me, for my Heavenly Father knows what I need even before I ask. I do not fear, for it is my Father's good pleasure to give me the kingdom.

I acknowledge that all my needs are met according to God's riches in glory by Christ Jesus. Grace and peace are multiplied unto me through the knowledge of God and of Jesus my Lord. His divine power has given me all things that pertain unto life and godliness, through the knowledge of Him that has called me to glory and virtue. Blessed be the God and Father of my Lord Jesus Christ, who has blessed me with every spiritual blessing in the heavenly places in Christ. The Lord is a sun and a shield to me and will give me grace and glory. No good thing will He withhold from me as I walk uprightly.

I choose to sow bountifully; therefore, I will reap bountifully. I give to the Lord, to His people, and to the needy as I purpose in my heart to give. I do not give grudgingly or out of compulsion, for my God loves a cheerful giver. God makes all grace abound towards me; I always have enough for all things, so that I may abound unto every good work.

The Lord supplies seed for me to sow and bread for my food. He also supplies and multiplies my seed for sowing and increases the fruits of my righteousness. I am enriched in everything unto great abundance, which brings much thanksgiving to God.

I bring all my tithes into the Lord's storehouse, so that there is meat in His house. As a result, He opens up the windows of heaven and pours out a blessing for me so that there is not room enough to contain it. He rebukes the devourer for my sake, so that he does not destroy the fruits of my ground and neither does my vine cast its grapes before the time. All the nations shall call me blessed, for I shall have a delightful life. I am blessed, because I consider the poor. Because I give freely to the poor, I will never want. My righteousness endures forever.

I remember the Lord my God, for it is He who gives me the power to make wealth, that He may confirm His covenant. Because Jesus Christ my Savior diligently listened to the voice of God and obeyed all the commandments, the Lord will set me high above all the nations of the earth and all the blessings in the kingdom shall come upon me and overtake me. Christ became poor so that through His poverty I might become rich.

Jesus came so that I would have life in its abundance. I am very blessed and favored of God and have been called to be a blessing to others.

## Scriptural References:

Matthew 6:33; Philippians 4:19; Luke 12:32; 2 Peter 1:2,3; Ephesians 1:3; Psalm 84:11; 2 Corinthians 8:9; 9:6-11; Psalm 41:1; Ps112:1a,9; Proverbs 28:27; Malachi 3:8-12; Deuteronomy 8:18; 28:1,22; John 10:10; Genesis 12:2

# DECREE
## For Christian Character

    I am the light of the world. A city set on a hill cannot be hid. I let my light so shine before men that they may see my good works and glorify my Father which is in heaven. Grace and peace are multiplied to me through the knowledge of God and of Jesus my Lord. His divine power has granted me everything that pertains to life and to godliness.

    He has given me exceeding great and precious promises. I live by these promises so that I might be a partaker of His divine nature, having escaped the corruption that is in the world through lust. Besides this, I give all diligence and add to my faith virtue, and to virtue knowledge, and to knowledge temperance, and to temperance patience and to patience godliness. To godliness, I add brotherly kindness and to brotherly kindness love. As these things are in me and abounding, I shall never be barren nor unfruitful in the knowledge of my Lord Jesus.

    I choose to walk worthy of the Lord in every respect, being fruitful in every good work and increasing in the knowledge of God. I give thanks to my Heavenly Father who has made me to be a partaker of the inheritance of the saints in light. He has delivered me from the power of darkness and has translated me to the kingdom of His dear Son, in whom

# DECREE

I have redemption through His blood, even the forgiveness of sin.

I am an imitator of God, as a dear child. I walk in love. Fornication and all uncleanness and covetousness have no part in my life, neither filthiness nor coarse jesting nor foolish talking, which are not fitting, but rather the giving of thanks. I let no corrupt communication proceed out of my mouth, but only that which is edifying, that it may minister grace to the hearers. I will not grieve the Holy Spirit of God whereby I have been sealed unto the day of redemption.

I choose to walk in lowliness of mind and esteem others as better than myself. I look not to my own interests but also to the interests of others. I make myself of no reputation and take the form of a bondservant.

I wait for the Lord and let integrity and uprightness preserve me. Jesus is a buckler to me, because I walk uprightly. I dwell on those things that are true, honorable, right, pure, lovely, of good repute, and excellent and worthy of praise.

As a child of God, I am thoroughly furnished for every good work. I consider how to provoke others to love. I put on a heart of compassion, kindness, humility, gentleness and patience, for I am God's workmanship, created in Christ Jesus for good deeds, which God prepared beforehand that I should walk in them.

I am patient and kind. I am not jealous. I do not brag and I am not arrogant. I do not act unbecomingly and do not seek my own way. I am not easily provoked and do not take into account a wrong suffered. I do not rejoice in unrighteousness, but rejoice with the truth. I bear all things, believe all things, hope all things and endure all things. The love of Jesus in me does not fail.

## For Christian Character

**SCRIPTURAL REFERENCES:**

Matthew 5:14-16; 2 Peter 1:2-8; Ephesians 2:10; 4:29,30; 5:1-5; Colossians 1:9-14; 3:12; Philippians 2:3-7; 4:8; 1 Corinthians 13:4-8; 2 Timothy 3:17; Hebrews 10:24

# DECREE
## For Spiritual Strength

I am strong in the Lord and in the strength of His might. I put on the full armor of God. In Christ I can do all things, because He strengthens me.

The Lord is my strength and my shield. My heart trusts in Him and I am helped; therefore my heart exults, and with my song I shall thank Him. He is my strength and my saving defense in time of trouble. The grace of the Lord Jesus Christ is with my spirit.

I build myself up in my holy faith, praying in the Holy Spirit. As I do this, I keep myself strong in the love of God. My God keeps me from falling and presents me faultless and blameless in the presence of my Heavenly Father with exceeding great joy.

My help comes from the Lord who made heaven and earth. He will not allow my foot to slip, and He who keeps me will not slumber. The Lord is my keeper. The Lord is my shade on my right hand. The sun does not smite me by day nor the moon by night. The Lord protects me from all evil. He keeps my soul, and He guards my going out and my coming in, from this time forth and forever.

When I pass through the valley of weeping, the Lord makes it a spring for me. I go from strength to strength in the

# DECREE

Lord. The Lord God is a sun and a shield to me. He gives me grace and glory, and no good thing does He withhold from me. I am blessed, because I trust in Him.

My Heavenly Father grants unto me, according to the riches of His glory, the ability to be strengthened with power through His Spirit in my inner man, so that Christ may dwell in my heart through faith and that I, being rooted and grounded in love, may be able to comprehend with all believers what is the breadth and length and height and depth and to know the love of Christ which surpasses knowledge, that I may be filled up to all the fullness of God.

I do not lose heart in doing good, for in due time I shall reap if I faint not. My eye is single, therefore my whole being is full of light. I am steadfast, immovable, always abounding in the work of the Lord, knowing that my toil is not in vain in the Lord. God is my strong fortress and He sets me in His way.

By Him, I can run through a troop and I can leap over a wall. He is a shield, because I take refuge in Him. He makes my feet like hinds' feet and sets me on my high places. He trains my hands for battle so that my arms can bend a bow of bronze. He has given me the shield of His salvation, and His help and strength make me great. I pursue my enemies and destroy them, because the Lord has girded me with strength for battle.

The Lord gives me strength when I am weary, and when I lack might, He increases power. I wait on the Lord and renew my strength. I mount up with wings like eagles. I run and do not get tired; I walk and do not faint.

## *For Spiritual Strength*

SCRIPTURAL REFERENCES:

Ephesians 6:10; Philippians 4:13; Psalm 28:7,8; 37:39; 84:5-7,11; 121; Philippians 4:23; Jude 1:20,21,24; Ephesians 3:16-19; Galatians 6:7-9; Matthew 6:22; 1 Corinthians 15:58; 2 Samuel 22:30-40; Isaiah 40:29-31

# DECREE
## Empowered to Go

I receive power when the Holy Spirit comes upon me to be the Lord's witness, even unto the uttermost parts of the earth. In Jesus' name, I go into all the world to preach the gospel to every creature.

These signs follow me as I go, because I believe: In the name of Jesus, I cast out devils, I speak with new tongues, I take up serpents, and if I drink any deadly poison, it shall not harm me. When I lay hands on the sick, they shall recover. I go forth and preach everywhere, and the Lord confirms the Word I preach with signs that follow. When I go, I go in the fullness of the blessing of the gospel of Christ.

The works that Jesus does, I do also in His name, and even greater works I do, because He has gone to the Father. Greater is He that is in me than he that is in the world. Jesus has given me power over all the power of the enemy. He has given me power over unclean spirits to cast them out and has enabled me to heal all manner of sickness and all manner of disease.

As I go, I will preach, saying, "The kingdom of heaven is at hand." I will heal the sick, cleanse the lepers, raise the dead. I will cast out devils. Freely I have received, so I will freely give. The Lord grants me boldness to speak His Word. He stretches out His hand towards me to heal and that signs and wonders may be done through the name of Jesus Christ. His Spirit has been poured out upon me and I prophesy.

All power in heaven and in earth has been given unto Jesus Christ. I will go in His name and teach all nations, baptizing them in the name of the Father, the Son and the Holy Spirit. I will teach them to observe all things that Jesus has taught me. Jesus is with me, even unto the end of the world. He has called me to Himself and has given me power and authority over all devils and to cure diseases. He has sent me to preach the kingdom of God and to heal the sick. As I go, Jesus prepares my way with His favor, for the Lord surrounds His righteous with favor as a shield. He sends His angels before me to watch over my ways and to bear me up lest I fall.

Like Jesus, I have been anointed with the Holy Spirit and with power. I go about doing good and healing all that are oppressed of the devil, for God is with me. He has anointed me to preach the gospel to the poor. He has sent me to proclaim release to the captives and recovery of sight to the blind, to set free all who are downtrodden and to proclaim the favorable year of the Lord.

I arise and shine, because my light has come and the glory of the Lord has risen upon me. Darkness shall cover the earth and gross darkness the peoples, but the Lord has risen upon me and His glory appears upon me. Nations will come to my light in Christ and kings to the brightness of my rising.

My speech and my preaching is not with enticing words of man's wisdom but in the demonstration of the Spirit and of power, that the faith of those I preach to should not stand on the wisdom of men, but in the power of God for the kingdom of God is not in word but in power.

## Empowered to Go

The Lord grants unto me, according to His riches in glory, to be strengthened with might by His Spirit in my inner man, according to His glorious power, unto all patience and longsuffering with joy. I labor according to His power that works mightily within me.

I preach not myself but Christ Jesus as Lord and myself as a bondservant of Christ and His Body, for Jesus' sake. For God who said, "Light shall shine out of darkness," is the One who has shone in our hearts to give the light of the knowledge of the glory of God in the face of Christ. I have this treasure in an earthen vessel, that the surpassing greatness of the power may be of God and not of myself.

Now unto the King eternal, immortal, invisible, the only wise God, who is able to do exceedingly abundantly above all that I could ask or think, according to the power that works within me, be honor and glory forever and ever. Amen.

### Scriptural References:

Acts 1:8; 10:38; Mark 16:15-21; Romans 15:29; John 14:12; 1 John 4:4; Luke 4:18; 10:1,2,19; Matthew 10:1,7; 28:18-20; Acts 4:29,30; Acts 2:17,18; Isaiah 60:1-3; Psalm 5:12; 91:11; 1 Corinthians 2:4; 4:19; Ephesians 3:16,20; Colossians 1:11,29; 2 Corinthians 4:5,6; 1 Timothy 1:17

# DECREE

## HEALTH AND HEALING

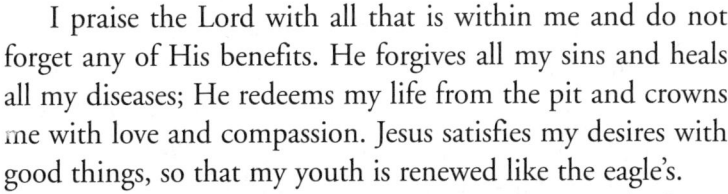

I praise the Lord with all that is within me and do not forget any of His benefits. He forgives all my sins and heals all my diseases; He redeems my life from the pit and crowns me with love and compassion. Jesus satisfies my desires with good things, so that my youth is renewed like the eagle's.

The Lord brings me to health and healing. He heals me and lets me enjoy abundant peace and security. The Sun of righteousness arises for me with healing in His wings, and I go out and leap like a calf released from the stall. Jesus bore my sins in His body on the cross, so that I might die to sin and live to righteousness. By His stripes I am healed. As my days are, so shall my strength be.

Jesus sent forth His Word and healed me; He rescued me from the grave. When I cry out, the Lord hears me; He delivers me from all my troubles. The Lord is close to me when I am broken-hearted and saves me when I am crushed in spirit. He has not given me a spirit of fear, but of love, power and a sound mind.

At times I may have many troubles, but the Lord delivers me from them all; He protects all my bones; not one of them will be broken. I am like an olive tree flourishing in the house of God; I trust in God's unfailing love forever and ever.

# DECREE

When the Lord's servants lay hands on me I recover, and when I am sick I call for the elders who pray over me, anointing me with oil in the name of the Lord. The prayer of faith saves me, and the Lord raises me up.

The law of the spirit of life in Christ Jesus has set me free from the law of sin and death. Jesus is the resurrection and the life. Because I believe in Him, I will live for all eternity. In Christ I live and move and have my being.

Because I dwell in the shelter of the Most High and rest in the shadow of the Almighty, I will say of the Lord, "He is my refuge and my fortress, my God, in whom I trust." Surely He will save me from the fowler's snare and from the deadly pestilence. He covers me with His feathers, and under His wings I find refuge; His faithfulness is my shield and rampart. I do not fear the terror of night, nor the arrow that flies by day, nor the pestilence that stalks in the darkness, nor the plague that destroys at midday. A thousand may fall at my side, ten thousand at my right hand, but they will not come near me. I will only observe with my eyes and see the punishment of the wicked. Because I make the Most High my dwelling—even the Lord, who is my refuge—then no harm will befall me, no disaster will come near my tent. He will command his angels concerning me to guard me in all my ways; they will lift me up in their hands so that I will not strike my foot against a stone. I will tread upon the lion and the cobra; I will trample the great lion and the serpent. Because I love the Lord, He will rescue and protect me from all accident, harm, sickness and disease. He is with me in trouble and delivers me. With long life He satisfies me and shows me His salvation.

Because I consider the poor; the Lord will deliver me in times of trouble. The Lord will protect me and keep me alive,

## Health and Healing

and I shall be blessed upon the earth. He will not give me over to the desire of my enemies. The Lord will sustain me upon my sickbed; in my illness, He will restore me to health.

**SCRIPTURE REFERENCES:**

Psalm 34:17-20; 41:1-3; 52:8; 103:1-3; 91; 107:20; Deuteronomy 33:25; Jeremiah 33:6; Malachi 4:2; 1 Peter 2:24; Deuteronomy 33:25; Romans 12:1; John 11:25,26; 2 Timothy 1:17; Mark 16:18; James 5:14,15

# DECREE

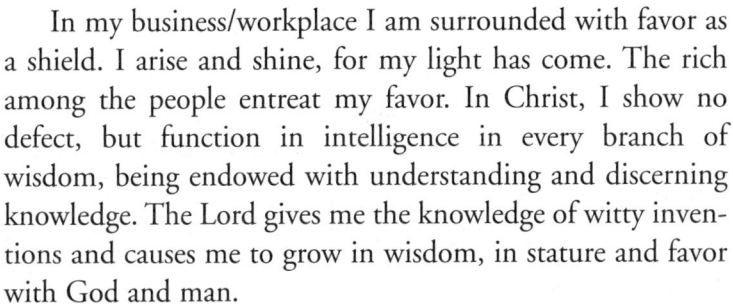

## For Business and the Workplace

In my business/workplace I am surrounded with favor as a shield. I arise and shine, for my light has come. The rich among the people entreat my favor. In Christ, I show no defect, but function in intelligence in every branch of wisdom, being endowed with understanding and discerning knowledge. The Lord gives me the knowledge of witty inventions and causes me to grow in wisdom, in stature and favor with God and man.

In my business/workplace, I am the head and not the tail. I am above and not beneath. The Lord commands blessings upon my business/workplace, and every project that I put my hands to prospers. He establishes my business and workplace as holy unto Himself.

My business/workplace does not submit to the Babylonian/world system, but instead submits to the kingdom of God and His righteousness. The integrity of the Lord guides me in my business. The Lord leans upon my business/workplace with regard and makes it fruitful, multiplying its productivity.

No weapon formed against my business/workplace prospers. Every tongue that rises up against it in judgement I condemn, and the Lord vindicates me. The Lord is a wall of fire around my business/workplace, and His glory is in the midst of it.

The Lord leads me by His presence, and He gives me rest. He makes goodness to pass before my business/workplace. His goodness and mercy follows me all the days of my life.

Peace, unity, love, integrity, honor and servanthood are godly values that prevail in my business/workplace.

I decree that Jesus Christ is Lord over my life, business and workplace!

### Scriptural References:

Psalm 5:12; Isaiah 60:1; Psalm 45:12; Daniel 1:4; Deuteronomy 28:1-13; Revelation 18:4; Proverbs 11:3; Leviticus 26:9; Isaiah 54:17; Zechariah 2:5; Exodus 33:14,19; Psalm 23:6

# DECREE
## For Family and Children

As for me and my family, we will serve the Lord. Because I believe in the Lord Jesus Christ, I shall be saved, and my entire house. Because I am a covenant child of God, my household is blessed. We have been blessed with every spiritual blessing in Christ. Blessings come upon us and overtake us.

My family, home, marriage and children are blessed, and all that I put my hands to do. I am blessed coming in, and I am blessed going out. The Lord has established my household as a people for Himself. He causes us to abound in prosperity, in the offspring of our bodies and the offspring of our beasts and the produce of our ground. The Lord surrounds my family and entire household with favor as a shield. No good thing does He withhold from us. His banner is love, over my home, marriage and family. No weapon formed against us as a family prospers. What the Lord has blessed, no man can curse. We abide in the shadow of the Almighty and no evil befalls us.

My children shall be mighty on the earth, for the generation of the upright are blessed. They shall be as signs and wonders in the earth.

My children will flourish like olive plants around my table. They are a gift from the Lord, and the fruit of the womb is my reward. My children are like arrows in the hand of a warrior. My sons in their youth are as grown-up plants and my daughters as corner pillars fashioned as for a palace.

Lord, Your covenant with me declares that Your Spirit which is upon me and Your words which You have put in my mouth shall not depart from my mouth, nor from the mouth of my children, nor from the mouth of my children's children. All my children shall be taught of the Lord, and great shall be their peace and prosperity. In righteousness they will be established, and they will be far from oppression. They will not be led into temptation, but they will know deliverance from evil. I confess that my children are pure in heart and therefore they shall see God. They hunger and thirst after righteousness, therefore they are filled. The Spirit of the Lord is poured out upon my children and they prophesy. The Lord's blessing is upon them. They will spring up among the grass like poplars by streams of water. One will say, "I am the Lord's," and another one will call on the name of Jacob, and another will write on his hand, "Belonging to the Lord."

I confess that my children are seekers of wisdom and understanding. They hold fast to Your Word and to Your ways. They treasure Your commandments, and they cry for discernment. The spirit of wisdom is poured out upon my children and my children's children, and words of wisdom are being made known to them.

The Lord keeps my family from falling and presents them blameless before the presence of the Father's glory with exceeding joy.

## For Family and Children

**SCRIPTURAL REFERENCES:**

Joshua 24:15; Acts 2:17; 16:31; Ephesians 1:3; Deuteronomy 28:1-12; Psalm 5:12; 84:11; 91:1,10; 112:2; 127:3,4; 128:3; 144:12; Song of Solomon 2:4; Isaiah 8:18; 59:21; 44:3-5; 54:13,14,17; Matthew 5:6,8; 6:13; Proverbs 1:23; 2:2,3; Jude 24

# DECREE
## Personal Decrees

# DECREE

## Personal Decrees

# DECREE

## *Personal Decrees*

# DECREE
## Notes

# DECREE

## Notes

# DECREE
## About the Author

**PATRICIA KING** is a passionate minister of Jesus Christ, serving as President of Christian Services Association (CSA) and Extreme Prophetic. Patricia is an internationally renowned speaker, television host, and prophetic minister who has authored numerous Bible courses, books and booklets.

www.extremeprophetic.com

## Other Resource Materials

Tapes, Books, CD's
by Patricia King
and other ministers

### Shop on-line

www.extremeprophetic.com